Spiritual Appetizers
for the SOUL

My Dear Sistah!
You are a TRAILBLAZER!
Keep leading the way.

LOVE
Ade
Oct 2023

ADE ANIFOWOSE

Copyright © 2022 Ade Anifowose

All rights reserved.

No part of this publication may be reproduced, distributed, or transmitted in any form or by any means, including photocopying, recording, or other electronic or mechanical methods, without the prior written permission of the publisher, except in the case of brief quotations embodied in critical reviews and certain other non-commercial uses permitted by copyright law.

For more information, contact
www.thebusinessofbeing.com

Cover Picture of drum by Ruth Schowalter

First Edition
ISBN: 979-8-372-98042-6

Published by:

Ancestral Stories

DEDICATION

Dedicated to those who are inspiring a revolution of love, self-acceptance, and the courage to dive deeper.

Be Still

Listen

Be Transformed

TABLE OF CONTENTS

Introduction 7

Spiritual Appetizers 11

Activate Your Consciousness 12

It's All About Love 31

Forgiveness Is Key 46

Healing Reveals The Soul 51

Yielding To Change 57

Tuning Into Connections 68

WOW – Words Of Wisdom 79

Acknowledgments 91

About The Author 93

Introduction

The picture of the drum on the front cover of this book is symbolic. I am a Sacred Drummer. My gift of drumming came from the deep well of my ancestral lineage. I was never taught how to play a Djembe drum. I just knew I could play it. It is a natural talent, a divine gift - a sacred gift.

Why am I telling you about my gift of drumming? Well, the messages in this book, I call them spiritual downloads, come from the same place as my gift of drumming. These messages are sacred. They are meant to align you with the rhythm of your soul. So that you can move and dance to the rhythm of your life. This may all sound metaphoric, but it is real. The language of the Soul is rooted in sound, music, rhythm, and vibration. The soul comes alive in metaphors. Life Itself is a metaphoric experience and an adventure. It calls for us to tune in to our soul and find our unique way; and live, dance, and express more abun-DANCE through our actions.

THERE IS A SONG INSIDE ME

There is a song inside you. Your song is uniquely yours. It will carry you through life's journey. Your song is ancient. It was placed in you by those who came before you. You are here to sing your song. Yearn for it daily. Let it sing through you. Desire it with an open heart, as you would a lover. Say Yes to it! Just for you, it will activate more harmony, more joy, and constant inspiration.

I am the perfect instrument for God's harmony. I am a healing love song. I am the music, the melody, and the lyrics. The rhythm of my soul guides my thoughts, inspires my actions, and heals my heart. The frequency of my song heals injustice, oppression, marginalization, and the sense of separation. I am a freedom song. I am a redemption song. Thank you, Order, in me, through me, as me, around me, through the Christ within. And so it is.

"Speaking to your souls in psalms and hymns and spiritual songs, sing with your heart to the Lord." Ephesians 5:19 Aramaic Version

Author: Ade Anifowose

Monday, September 26, 2022

Copyright: Hillside International Truth Center, Inc.

(Used with permission.)

Spiritual Appetizer anyone?

Sometimes, in this busy world that we have created, we need a quick shot of inspiration to re-energize and reactivate what is important to us. Other times when we sit to meditate, we just might need an inspirational thought to anchor into. "*Spiritual Appetizers for the Soul*" is for these moments.

These messages were received over several years, during meditation, contemplation, while hosting my radio shows, podcast episodes, and sometimes in moments when my conscious mind was distracted by challenging situations, pain, and struggles… suddenly, spiritual truth dropped into my awareness.

Some of these downloads were shared on social media in the early stages. After a long journey of anguish, frustration, surrender, breathing, and pushing, it is finally here….

I live my life based on the foundation stones that inspired these downloads. You can meditate on them. You can open a page in the middle of a project, at home, at work, or at any moment in time - when you are feeling misaligned. When you wake up in the morning or when you are going to bed. Take a deep breath and open to a page and let the spirit of the messages speak to you. Let the messages reconnect you with the wisdom of your soul. Let them inspire the best and highest in and through you. And let them remind you that:

You are worthy.

You have value.

You belong.

YOU ARE ENOUGH!

There are times you might find that the messages hit the spot. Other times, you might be resistant. When this occurs, take a deep breath, and another breath… and another. Then ask, "What am I resisting?" Listen. Trust what you hear and/or feel. No judgment. Just listen and let it be.

This way of being opens your heart and mind to catch a "new thought." A new thought inspires a new way of seeing and being in the world.

Go ahead, open to a page now and listen to what your soul has to say to you right now.

Spiritual Appetizers

We are vibrational beings.
We are energy in action.
All of life is energy.
This energy responds to our every thought.
Your thoughts are energy in motion.

This is the divine connection.

What You FOCUS on,
You ACTIVATE.

What You ACTIVATE,
You RADIATE.

What You RADIATE,
You ATTRACT.

What You ATTRACT
Becomes
Your REALITY!

What are you focusing on right now?
Is this the reality you desire?

Breathe.

Activate Your Consciousness

Surrender to LOVE.
Forgive the past.
Find your voice.
Live your truth.

Say YES to your gift!
It is your meal ticket.
Release it and receive much more.

Sacred Truth.
Life is a never-ending story.
The story of the No-Thing
that became Some-thing.

What is *your* role?!

Play, Love, Laugh, Cry, Inspire, Share.
Be of service and stay tuned
to the soul-full director of your Story.

How far do you want to go in life?

Unwrap your gifts and let yourself travel beyond your wildest dreams.

Your gifts are the keys to your blessings.
They will take you to places that were once figments of your imagination.
You will sit face to face with people who were once
mentors from afar.

Your gifts will always make room for you
and put you
in the presence of exceptional people.

You deserve all the good that life has to offer.
It is your birthright.

There is nothing you have ever done or will ever do
that can change this truth.
God's will for you is to live
a life of joy, happiness, perfect health, abundance, and *so* much more.
You just have to allow it
by remembering
it is your birthright.

---◆---

When you are *listening* to something
so strong within you,
no matter what happens,
your YES will keep you moving forward.

Do you have the courage
to *sing*
your heart song,
even if the stage of life is scary?

---◆---

When you are not at peace with your family,
you are not at peace with yourself.
All of humanity is *inter-connected.*
The connection between you and your family
is one of life's strongest bonds.
There is nothing you can do to sever that
connection.
You and your family are connected
just like branches are connected to the tree trunk
and a tree to its roots.
When there is discord or dis-ease in one part of the
tree,
other parts of the tree are affected.
If you are willing to heal the discord,
the first step is to surrender.
You surrender to dealing with the discord,
this is love,
which opens the door to healing.

Know that your soul has the answer.
Listen to the answer.
Live the answer.
Be the answer.

Your heart is your GPS.
Listen to its guidance.

Your heart is the doorway
to all that makes you come alive.
When you listen to her guidance,
you will be led back to your true Self.

Listen to her.
Fall in love with her.

She loves you unconditionally.
She will set you on fire and
transform your life.

It takes courage to surrender.

Spiritual surrender is yielding to the good
that is already yours.

When you surrender, you are surrendering to
Divine Intelligence.

Activate Your Consciousness

Use your energy for good.
Your life depends on it.
When you focus on using your energy for good,
the benefits are everlasting.
Your view of life will be affirming.
You will trust life more.
You will *know* that you
live in a friendly universe.

Your relationships will reflect harmony.
Your body will radiate goodness.
Emotionally,
you will know contentment.
Mentally,
you will know stillness and peace of mind.

What you give always comes back to you.
You only get to keep what you give away.
It is a universal law.

All roads lead to Mother-Father God.
Relax, you are not lost or stuck.
Everything is always in motion,
and so are you.
Your current location is the path to
Mother-Father God.

The path *is* Mother-Father God, period!
Mother-Father God is the road,

the path, the destination, the beginning, and the end.
The end is a new beginning.
Take a breath.

The heart thrives in a space of stillness.
Be still.
Be in your heart.

Roar with passion
and watch fear shatter
like glass
into a million pieces.
Passion is vibrationally higher than fear.
When you live from a passionate state,
you come alive.
You become light.

Where there is light, darkness disappears.
Where there is light, fear cannot exist.
Align with your passion,
and commit each day
to live in, from, and through
your passion.

Re-lease Yourself.
You own nothing.
Look around you.
Do you really own anything?
Go deeper. Think about it.
Everything is temporary.

Even your existence on this planet is temporary.
The one thing that you take with you
wherever you go
is your consciousness.

How you live your life is up to *you*.

You are responsible for *you* -
your happiness, joy, and peace of mind.

Set yourself free of circumstances
that are holding you hostage,
preventing you from
moving forward in life.

Return, trade-in, or release
what is no longer working for you and
start anew.

Set yourself free.

Stop running from what you want
because you are worried
about what you don't have.

Every idea has within it the means to attract what
you need to fulfill it.

Thankfully, we are not privy to the end results of
our dreams, goals, and visions.

If we were, chances are we might be intimidated
by what we see and/or be attached to what it is
going to look like.

Whatever knowledge, gifts, and talents
you have
are meant to be used.
Life will supply your needs.
Don't be like a fish in water,
swimming around looking for water.
You are surrounded
by all you need,
right now.
Know this.
Live this.
Take action and continue to take action.
Action is transformative.

Life is a hero's journey,
with many dragons to slay.

The dragons appear in many forms.
Ultimately, the dragons are within.
The dragons
may cause you to run
in the opposite direction
of where
your soul is leading you.

When you feel the nudge of the dream in your heart,
don't run in the opposite direction,
don't ignore the nudges.
Ignoring them doesn't make them go away.
It can actually leave you feeling
depressed, sad, and unfulfilled
if you ignore the nudges.
There is an internal unrest
when you ignore
or deny
your soul's urge to create.

You see,
the urge is pointing you in the direction
of what you are on this earth to birth.
Pay attention.
Be in the now.
This deep call
from within

is a call you must answer,
and the fact that you can
see, hear, and feel it
lets you know
you are equipped to make it happen.

Can you imagine a fish saying,
"I know I can swim,
but where is the water?"
The water is all around the fish.
The water is part of its life,
so close that they are inseparable.
Today, like a fish,
I ask you to swim – move,
take a small step,
and let Life support your movement.

Trust the moment and know God's Power within you
is guiding your every step and action.
Go for it! Don't wait! Do it now!

Activate Your Consciousness

Welcome vulnerability.

Let life in.
You are perfectly designed to handle
all that Life has for you.

Surrender!
Open up and be lifted up!

There is an invisible
Spiritual stuff
all around us.

Everything that was created was created out of this
stuff.

It is a Spiritual Substance.

Grab some and create your reality.

Use your power of imagination
to mold and create what you desire.

Have fun with this "Spiritual Playdough."

Stay open.

Stay awake.

Stay young.

You matter!
You are here to stand out.
Don't compromise.

Life is good
and it is getting better.
Let it.

Let go of what isn't working for you
and watch a new reality appear before you.

The moment you let go,
you gain new meaning.

Stop tripping.
Why trip,
when you can trust?

Trust that there is
a better perspective in the periphery
of your consciousness.

L O L

It is time to
LAUGH out LOUD.
It is time to
LIVE out LOUD.
It is time to
LOVE out LOUD!!!
The time is now!
Do it . . . NOW!

You are not stuck.

You are holding on.

Let go. Be free!

Life is in motion, and so are you.
Everything is active and in motion.
Whenever you are feeling stuck,
be aware that
you are thinking the same thought
over and over
about your situation.

Choose a new thought,
change your perspective,
and get back into the flow of Life.

Grow with the flow!

Show up
and
BE the cause.

Just Be-cause!

You Are It!

Choose this day to celebrate the
Christ Consciousness within you . . .

It is your *true* essence.

It is your spiritual identity.

Say YES to your life!

Why beat yourself down
when you have the power
to lift yourself up?

Happy remembrance of
who you *truly* are.
One with the Divine.
One with God/Goddess.
One with the *all* Good of Life!

The *old* has been crossed out and
the *new* you is shining through.
Welcome Home!

You are ALIVE!!!

You are already success-full.
Your mission is to discover and uncover the
success that is already within you.

Success is within you because it is your birthright.

Do you know you are here on this planet
to fulfill a unique mission?
Only you can fulfill this mission.
This means that your chance of success is 100%
guaranteed.
You must refuse the urge
to compare your mission to others.
Stay focused.

Let go of needing something to fall back on and
let your vision pull you up… higher.

Tune in or
Be tuned out.

Tune in or
miss out on
divine guidance.

There is a song in the ethers for you.
Your innate gift is the
instrument to bring it into being.

So, sing *your* song!

Instead of choosing to be afraid,
choose to be amazed!

At least, be curious.

Catch the vibe.
BE the vibe!
Live the vibe!!
Raise your vibe!!!

You are not *a part* of God.
You are *all* of God.
God in the flesh.

Breakdown is part of the process
of spiritual growth.
With every breakdown,
there is a *break through*.
Embrace it and
break free.

Healing can be messy and scary sometimes.
During the messy moments,
it is the perfect opportunity to
let go of erroneous beliefs.
Say YES to more of God.
YES, to more of the good
that is seeking to express through and as you.

Say YES!

Just for today:

Don't tell God what you want.
Listen to what God has for you.

Just for today.

It's All About Love

LOVE

It is time to go back to the beginning
to re-learn, to re-teach yourself
what Love really is.

Love is more than what can be taught.
It is an experience.

Love is more than words.
It is high vibrational energy.

Your thoughts and words of Love must translate
into action
in order for Love to be made visible.

When Love is expressed through your action,
it is recognized and felt.

It heals.

In the presence of Love, you are free.
To know Love as freedom,
you have to set free
the demands, you put on Love.
The demands you put on Love become
the demands you place on yourself.

The limitations you put on Love
are also revealed
when you are in love or making love.
When the act of love is conditional,
you limit Love and your experiences of Love.
In order to know Love as freedom,
you have to free Love and freely love!

True Love is everywhere present.
It is the harmonizing force that holds all things
together.

True Love is unconditional,
and it is freely available right now,
right where you are.

Get still.
Take deep breaths.
Listen to the song of your heart.
In stillness,
you align with the presence of Love.

Calling all lonely hearts!!!
Don't be afraid of intimacy.
It is what we all desire- heart-to-heart connections.

We *all* belong,
and we are *all* longing
for each other.
Dropping the idea that we are separated from each other returns us to our innate sense of connection with the *All That Is*.
Everyone and everything is connected.

Surrender to the connection.
Surrender to Life
Surrender to LOVE!

Stand your ground
for
Love and transformation!

Love is the most powerful force
in the Universe.
It is an attractive force.
It holds everything together.

Standing for Love and transformation
is why you are here on this planet.
You are an earth angel here to remind others
what Love looks like.
You are here to be love
in the midst of the seeming lack of Love.
Where there is Love,
there is belonging and connection.

With this understanding,
we re-cognize
our brotherhood and sisterhood.

Love melts the hardening of the heart,
heals hurts, and woundedness.
Your commitment to Love
becomes the healing medicine
that transforms how you see

yourself and others.
Standing for Love and transformation
is the work of an enlightened soul.

You are it!

The best way to play
the game of life
is to stick to the
"script" of *your* life.
The script of your life is a love story.
The story of ups and downs,
ebbs and flows,
mistakes and retakes,
discovering and uncovering.
The story of triumphs
in spite and because of all the challenges
you have experienced.
You are the protagonist of your movie.
Love is your Director.
Listen and follow its direction.
Choose Love.
Be love.
Be loving!

Love wins.

If there ever was an "original" sin,
it would be hate.

Hate is rooted in separation.
Hate is believing
that we are separated from one another,
that we can be separated from God.

When this belief informs your actions,
your view of life is of lack,
limitation, greed, judgment, and criticism.

Everything and everyone are interconnected.
Love is the unifying energy that reminds you
that you are connected
to all of life.
In Love, hate ceases to exist.
Life looks brighter,
and there is a sense of knowing that
you are connected to others.
You feel you are a part
of a soul family.
Togetherness is natural.
Let Love take you deeper to the core
of divine unification.

Love is freedom.
We experience that freedom when we
love without conditions.

Have you ever considered
doing what you love
freely,
joyfully,
without demanding payment?

Do you know
that you are
loving
when you use your gifts and talents?

Do you know
that you are
blocking your own good
when you don't share
your gifts and talents
unless someone is going to pay for them?

Placing demands
on how you share your gifts and talents
is conditional love.
Conditional love is restrictive
and
everyone misses out on the good
that wants to be birthed through you.

The same is true when you give of yourself, and you are not open to receiving because you do not value your gifts and talents.

How can you give of yourself today?

Are you willing to open to more love than you have ever imagined?

Commit to giving of yourself.
Share your gifts and talents.

Herein lies your freedom,
joy, and peace of mind.

Say YES to Love;
and
share your gifts and talents.

You will be blessed abundantly.

It is time for your "*Regular Love Check Up*".

You are scheduled for
re-learning
and
re-membering
what Love really is.

Spiritual Appetizers for the Soul

This is an opportunity
for you
to uplevel your lovability,
instead of living by other people's definitions of
Love.

Check in.
Be renewed.

Sometimes we hold Love hostage
for fear of being judged, ridiculed, or hurt.

We wait until we think it is *safe* to hug,
give a word of encouragement,
stand up for what is right,
or speak up in the face of injustice.

Show up for Love.
Free Love.
Freely love… you!

Love BE-ings
BE Love,
recognize it is the essence of
who you are.

DO Love,
extend the essence of
who you are

through your actions.

Then you will HAVE Love,
as you recognize that
YOU are LOVE!

What is Love?
I can show you
through my actions.
However, it is better to find out for yourself.

You will know Love by how much you are willing
to open your heart.

To really know Love,
Are you willing to have your heart broken open?

Betrayal,
disappointments, grief, and vulnerability
will break you open to *feel* deeply.
It is all part of the process of
spiritual maturity,
if you choose it to be so.

Love is eternal.
Everything else will perish.
Everything that you can see and touch
will one day perish and disappear.
Love will always be present.
Love was pre-sent before you appeared as a
human incarnation of the Great I Am.
Love transcends time and space.

When you fall in love with yourself,
others have no choice
but to fall in love with you.
If they don't,
it won't matter,
because you will be busy
loving your life
and
living the life you love.

Some people say,
"I love you."
Some say it and live it.
Some show it by their actions.
Let your actions be infused with Love.

Spiritual appetizers for women.

When we celebrate mothers,
do not allow yourself to be disillusioned by thinking
because you didn't birth a child through your womb,
you are not a mother.

The truth is,
every woman is a mother;
in fact, we all are mothers.
We are all birthing divine ideas of God/Goddess
every day,
in every way.

Celebrate the Divine Feminine
that is within you.
Continue to be the giver of love.
Be the space and place where Mother-Father God
gets to re-present Itself.

The Universe is always making love with anyone
who is open and receptive,
and it is generous with its love-making.
Every time you catch an idea that inspires,
every time you taste

the most delicious food,
every time you see a picture
or scene that takes your breath away,
you are making love with the Universe.

When you stay aligned, open, and receptive,
you give yourself permission
to tap into Universal Love.

Suffering,
when met
with presence and awareness,
can lead to a place and space
of compassion.

Compassion
for what you are growing through
and compassion
for the journey of your life.

In essence, compassion is
a gift bestowed by suffering,
if we choose it to be a gift.
This compassion naturally enfolds
us and others - directly and indirectly.

It's All About Love

When you resist the present moment,
you block your own healing.
You resist your ability to be fully alive,
to *feel* fully alive and awake.
The present moment is invigorating.
It is grounding
and affords you a deeper perspective on life,
and who and what you are.

If you think Love is weak -
You are *asleep*.
If you think Love isn't everything –
You might be *confused*.
If you think Love is only passion,
you don't know who you really are.

So, what is Love, you ask?
YOU are…Love!

When you know this, *really* know it,
your life and legacy will be a love song,
a song of freedom.
A redemption song.
and
the chorus will be something like this:
"Love is all there is.
I am free.
I am the answer."

Love is the glue that holds everything together.
It is okay to surrender to it.
Love's got your back.
Love is self-sustaining.
Trust it.

Forgiveness Is Key

Forgiveness clears the path to wholeness.
Wholeness is your birthright.
If you are feeling less than whole,
it is time to release
an erroneous habit, belief, thought, or idea about
yourself or another.

Forgiveness is a choice.
A choice to choose to live.
Forgiveness is the healing of your pain – physical,
emotional, mental, and spiritual.
Forgiveness is to your heart and mind
what bathing is to your physical body.
It is a cleansing ritual
that transcends right or wrong.
It returns you to the One.
The Great I Am.

Forgiveness frees you up to fully live.
It is not a condoning of another's action.
It is choosing to be free,
to let go of what no longer serves you.
Making room in your heart and mind for Love to heal you.

Forgiveness is a healing medicine
for your soul, spirit, mind, and body.
You have the power to set yourself free.
Choose to be healed.
Choose wholeness.
Choose forgiveness.
Today!

Life is not for wimps.
It is full of ups and downs.
There are times when you are not even sure
what is going on.
So much is happening at once.
You are not sure if you are coming or going.
Somehow, you always find the strength
to keep moving.

While life is not for wimps,
a spiritual path is for "heart-centered gladiators."

Forgiveness Is Key

A spiritual path
is a unique path designed
for your soul's evolution,
one that requires you
to stay awake, aware,
and be an active participant
in the unfolding of your life.

Waking up and taking responsibility
for one's action
is the path to inner freedom.

When people push your button,
thank them.
They are reminding you
to turn on
the light of Love,
the light of Truth that you are.
Your light
will dissolve all discords
and bring a new understanding
to your triggers and frustrations.

Freely embrace Love.
Forgiveness is the choice
to FREE yourself
and EMBRACE the LOVE
that is all around you.

Forgive and receive Love!
Be the cause of what you desire,
And the effect will show up
Be-cause you have the power to create and recreate.

We are all equal and different.
Celebrate it.
Accept it.
Embrace it.
This is the way of Love.

Considering how judgmental and critical humans can be,
it is no surprise that we struggle
with unconditional Love.
Every day, we are all challenged
to learn what unconditional Love is . . . .

The thing is it is really easy
to put the lesson on hold,
on a rain check, or we respond
to the invitation of unconditional Love
with the same old mindset
of fear, judgment, blame, criticism, shame, or guilt.

When the response is openness
and a willingness to understand,
we are met
with a new kind of interaction.

With understanding comes compassion.
Compassion is the pathway
to unconditional Love.

Being authentic
doesn't mean being perfect.
It means being perfectly you.
It means giving yourself permission
to be free . . .
Free to see perfection
in perceived imperfection.

Choose freedom today!
Let it all hang out!
The most important person
who needs to love it all
is *you*.
Be free!!

Healing Reveals The Soul

There is no healing without being vulnerable.
Healing is the process of clearing
and releasing of stagnated energy.

Old, unresolved emotions block the flow
of your life energy,
causing depression, sadness, and dis-ease
to name a few.

Old emotions must be released
for you to heal.
If not released,
they remain stuck in the body,
leaving you feeling
overwhelmed and depressed.

Real healing invites you to open yourself
to the truth- *raw authentic truth.*
Whatever is causing you pain,
spiritually, emotionally, mentally, or physically.
Bring it all to the altar of transformation.

Telling the truth opens the door to self-affirmation.
In speaking *your* truth about your pain, hurt, disappointment, betrayal, and/or abuse,
you honor yourself,
your life journey,
and begin the process to
reclaim your power
from moment to moment.
Remember,
within your vulnerability
is your healing and strength.
Have the courage to show up for *You*!

Don't suppress your tears.
When you need to cry, cry!

Tears help you express emotions for which there are no words.

Do you consider crying as a sign of weakness?
Think again!

Consider your tears as healing,
cleansing water
for your soul, heart,
mind, and body.

When life is too much to bear,
when the emotion of grief
is strangling your peace of mind,
tears release the emotional pressure.

Your tears are expressions of your soul.
It takes courage to cry
and not be ashamed
in a world
where expression of pain and vulnerability
are considered weakness.
Go ahead;
honor your soul.

Intimate Relationships
are the highest forms
of spiritual practice
next to parenting.
Breathe!

An intimate relationship, specifically,
a romantic relationship offers you
the opportunity
to heal past childhood traumas
in the present.

With this awareness,
you can change the dynamic
of your relationship.
You can release
your beloved
from the wrath of your projection
by finding faults, blaming, and/or criticizing.

Be gentle.
When the tide (of emotions) is rising.
Be willing to surf the "ocean of emotions."
When it gets rough,
reach out, literally and metaphorically, to hold the hands of your beloved.

Keep your mind and heart open
and rest in the healing power of understanding,
self-care, and compassion.
Steady and easy does it.

Every relationship is a tool to help you discover yourself,
on a deeper level.
You are in a relationship with everyone and everything - directly and indirectly.
Without relationships,
how would you know who you are?

Relationships are mirrors.
They help us see who we are.
Everything and everyone
reflects who we are.
We are all here to
relate-on-the-ship called, Life.

Your life is a miracle.
Think about it.
You are God in action.
BE grateful!

Life has no opposite.
Give up the fight.
Welcome the moment.

Don't let the confusion
of others cloud your clarity.

Healing is messy!
Stay present.
Release the urge to judge
what you are feeling and the situation.
Your awareness in that moment will bring about
the healing your soul desires.

Yielding To Change

The fear of change
leaves you creating
the same old unpleasant experiences
in your life.

Everything is energy.
The thoughts we hold
broadcast into the ethers
and attract similar thought vibrations.

Whatever thought you hold
becomes the filter through
which you experience the world.

If you have a desire to grow and expand,
you are welcoming change.

There is no growth without change.
Change and growth are synonymous.
Fear of change
is focusing on what you do not want.

Change is your ally.
It is your "Prayer Partner."

When change is occurring,
your prayers are being answered.

See your life with a fresh new perspective
and consciously accept
what shows up
in your experience.

Be willing to step
into a new space and place in consciousness
and know that the change
is happening for your good.

The key is to welcome peace
right where you are.

Do you want to change?
Really?!
Then, let go!

You are the one
holding on
to the safety net of old paradigms.

When you come up
against an opportunity to grow,
say Yes!

Open yourself up to Divine Guidance.

For example, the guidance could nudge you to do the opposite of what you would normally do.

If you have been afraid to have a long overdue conversation
with someone, do it.

If a friend invites you out,
and you normally would turn down the invitation,
accept it.

The point of this exercise is to create
a different experience in your life.
A different way of being.

Just for today, experiment with the idea of saying,
Yes!

Say YES,
when you are prone to say no,

Say No,
when yes is usually the unconscious default response.

The answer to your deeper questions
is always LOVE!
Surrender to it.

Love rocks and Love rules!!

Yielding To Change

People only defend
what they believe to be true,
even if it is inaccurate.
Sometimes, they defend what they haven't
accepted as true for themselves, just because of
their attachment to being right.

When you find yourself defending
a point of view,
ask yourself:

What am I defending?
Why am I defending it?
What am I afraid of seeing?
What would I lose or gain
if I surrender to a different point of view?

Spiritual Truth needs no defense.
When you understand the spiritual laws
that govern Life
and who you *really* are,
you will recognize
that there is no need to be defensive.
You become
a force to be reckoned with.
As you move through life with openness.

A deeper understanding of Life
and who and what you are
makes you
flexible,
adaptable,
and strong enough
to inspire change
while opening yourself up to more.

Life experiences,
such as trauma, grief, or loss,
offer you a gift, a unique depth into your life.
If you cultivate the courage
to unwrap the gifts,
they can make you better, not bitter.

We are here to deliver Love.
We are here to remember ourselves
as Love embodied.
When we open our hearts,
we have an opportunity to get in touch
with who and what we *really* are.

I don't believe that when we open our hearts,
we are going to be a target for negativity.

Sure, people might be triggered
by their own insecurities
when our light
is shining on their darkness.
If they react to our expression of love
in a way that seems negative,
we can recognize that it is their pain speaking.
It is a call for love.
Like a moth to a flame,
"insecurity" is always attracted to the security of love.
Will you *be* love in the presence of negativity?

We all have the ability to live from a heart-centered space.
Some find it easier, maybe safer, to live from a head-centered (egoic) space.
Let your heart guide your ego.
The wisdom of the heart knows the way.

Spiritual growth and
development
are processes of remembering.
We discover who we are.
Embrace the courage to be ourselves
and be true to our (higher) Self.
This is our birthright.

Reconnect with your inner child.
With Love as your refuge, it will be a great reunion.
A return to Love.

Become so drunk with Love
that you don't even recognize negativity,
so drunk that your love
wards off and transforms any negativity
and attracts more of what lights you up.
The energy you put out into the world,
you attract into *your* world.

Love is your protection.
Go forth and *be* love in action.
Let Love be.
This is your mission.

Yielding To Change

When you are ready to make your transition
into the spirit realm,
how will you answer this question?
"How did you love?"

Your reason for being is to love out loud!

If you desire growth,
relationships are the best fertilizer.
Especially the ones that smell like manure.
Breathe!
Yes, breathe!

Choosing freedom is choosing
to know yourself
and
be yourself.
It is a lifelong adventure.
Be easy
as you move through your journey.

The Birthing of A New Love

I was married to "Always Working,"
but she was too much.
She didn't even want
my last name.
So I started seeing this new lady, called, "Rest."
She is cool!
Easy-going, no drama, and
she makes me feel really good.
"Always Working"
was high maintenance.
"Rest" is from a great family called Love.
I love her whole family,
and I fit right in.
When I am hanging out with
her and her family,
I am at peace,
inspired, and creative.

Gotta go . . .
I have a date with "Rest."

When you catch *inspiration* and
add a little bit of *action*,
you have, *creation*.

If you are struggling to get to a place
to do what you love,
start by loving
what you are doing.
The consciousness that obtains, sustains.
Welcome Love now!

Love what you are doing now,
and love will guide and sustain it.

If a mindset of struggle is your natural default,
your mind has been programmed to accept
struggle as the path to achievements.

Choose again.
Think a new thought.
Let life support you.

Once you embrace the Truth,
all lies will dissolve and disappear.

---◆---

Mistakes are an important part of life.
When you make a mistake,
ask to see the "gift"
being offered by the mistake.

---◆---

A mistake is nothing more than a "missed-take."
When this happens,
remind yourself that
you didn't do anything wrong.
It's just a mistake.

Be the Director of your movie and joyfully call out,
"Take 2, Take 3, heck, Take 1000 . . ."
Try something new.
It is *your* movie!

Oh, one more thing,
when you stop making mistakes,
you are no longer learning.
Mistakes are opportunities
to learn something new.
Embrace yourself, your journey,
and embrace Life.

---◆---

Tuning Into Connections

———◆———

The Ego talks!
The Heart listens!!

The ego's information
is based on past experiences and separation.
Its job is to keep you in check,
to stay within the confines of your comfort zone.
And make sure you do the "right" thing
based on old conditioning - societal,
religious, socio-economic, cultural,
political, racial conditioning, etc.
In the name of "protection,"
it shields you from what may be
perceived as harmful and
what threatens its existence.
If your ego is running the show, you will continue
to react to life habitually.

Align with your heart
and learn
a new way of being.

Trust the wisdom of your heart.

———◆———

Spiritual Appetizers for the Soul

Check in with yourself regularly, and ask if
your point of view is more ego-based
or heart-centered.

Someone operating mainly from ego
is primarily interested in being right and/or in control,
rather than allowing themselves
to step into the world of another person.

When you develop the ability to listen,
really listen, to what someone is saying,
this is an act of love.
You become a healing space.
A healing space for the person to feel heard.
You grow and
the level of intimacy deepens.
You realize that there is nothing to defend.
You become a space for love and healing.

Your heart is the gateway
to the wisdom of the ages.
It transcends time and space.
When you live from your heart,
you connect to the sound of your soul.

Imagine a world where we *intentionally* listen
to what another person is saying,
instead of impatiently waiting to reply
or to make them wrong.

What is possible?

No matter how you perceive yourself,
you are part of a Divine Plan.
Always was.
Always is.
Always will be!

Relax, you are in Good/God's hands.

Be Still.

In stillness,
you remember who you are,
your purpose,
and your greatness.
You are God's Plan in action.

Accept this truth.

Your existence is as important
as every heartbeat.
Trust the quiet nudges.

Trust your heart.
Trust Life.
Life is for you, never against you.

Breathe . . .

True Justice creates a space for everyone to win.
Where there is justice, there is harmony.
True justice arises from the heart.
True justice is a commitment
to restoration, repair, and healing.

True justice is an invitation to open to something
beyond the norm.
It asks those involved
to be open and available
to a new understanding, and possibility.

True justice is alive, dynamic,
and
it is *all-inclusive!*

Hiding who you are perpetuates insecurity.

Your security
is in your authenticity.

We are all unique
and our individual uniqueness
is what adds beauty to the world.

When you live in your authenticity,
you access *your* power.
You are plugged in.
You are turned on.

Your authenticity activates
a deep listening within you.
You hear, see, and think differently.
You recognize that you are a
"Creative Misfit,"
never born to fit in
but to stand out
and be seen
because you matter.

Authenticity energizes your security.

Until you learn to be secure
about your own insecurities,
you will not be able
to create
a sacred space for others
to be with their own insecurities.

You are a "Soul Gardener"
planting seeds of transformation, self-acceptance,
love, kindness,
service, and community.
Keep plowing, planting, and producing.
You are guaranteed
to reap how you have sown.

Being authentic reconnects
you with your *true* power.

When you are true to yourself,
you give yourself permission
to reveal the good,
the bad, the ugly, and the
"I can't even talk about it!"
You give yourself permission –
permission to embrace
all of *you*.

Tuning Into Connections

This is not permission to be unkind to others;
it is permission to recognize
your own pain, wounds, triumphs, worthiness, and value.

Being authentic is a choice to live aligned with
your heart and soul.
It empowers you to hold space for the
healing of your trauma and whatever you consider
to be negativity.

Your authentic power will dissolve
shame and guilt.

Being authentic is permission to embrace
what is magnificent about you,
your uniqueness, beauty, creativity,
and the fact that you exist.

This is authenticity –
a willingness to embrace *your* humanity.

You are here!
You belong!

Spiritual Appetizers for the Soul

There is a natural state of being.
When you stop
and focus your attention
on the present moment,
you will sense it.
Take some time
to be still and listen
to the stillness
within you.
Cultivate a consciousness of stillness.
This aligns you
with the natural flow
of abundance
in you and around you.
Your natural state is… BEing.

Your past is the stepping stone
to your future.
Rather than curse or fear your past,
recognize that your past has brought you
to where you are today.

Tuning Into Connections

Every step counts.
Every moment will serve to lift you higher
if you choose
to see from a broader perspective.

Surrender to now and RISE!

Until you embrace the "mess" in your life,
you won't receive the "message."
And you can't *be* a "messenger" of Love.

Do you want to be a messenger of Love?
Learn to embrace your mess.

Sit with it long enough
to receive its message.

There is so much you can learn
when you take an honest look at the so-called,
mess in your life.

It is easy to sweep your
mess under the rug or blame someone for the
mess.

Great insight can emerge
from your messiness.

The next time you discover

a mess in your life,
stay open,
a message is about to be delivered.
This is all part of your initiation as a messenger of Love.

The real you is so much more beautiful than the made up you.
The real you is powerful, intelligent, smart, funny, loving, grounded, and embracing of life.

Really, there are not enough adjectives to describe the real you.
Spend some time with the real you, and
you will be inspired by you!

Loneliness and neediness are the echoes
of deep longing . . .
to feel loved,
to belong,
to know we are needed.
It is an innate recognition
of our connection to each other.

When this "need" to connect
is not met or acknowledged
by those around us
or our community,

we feel abandoned - lonely.

Be with your feelings and emotions.
Don't try to change your feelings and emotions.
Make space.
Be the witness to your own sense of vulnerability
and tenderness.
You will be guided on what to do next.
Trust the wisdom within.

We are all Doctors of Philosophy (PhD).
We are
Pure,
Holy,
and
Divine.

WOW – Words Of Wisdom

Be You.
Do You.
Have You.
Love You.

SOCIAL AWARENESS

It can be fun to TWEET your thoughts and share your FACE, INSTANTLY, but don't forget to PIN point what is important to YOU!

Remember that your life is a STREAM of consciousness,
that finds meaning when you SHARE it . . . .

It is time to let your godness HANGOUT
and be a beneficial presence,
SOCIALLY.
Keep this in the INBOX of your mind.
It will be your DIRECT MESSAGE to your heart-song, purpose, truth, and liberation.

Do not allow your challenges
to fog up your clear understanding
of who you *really* are.
The challenges are strengthening processes
that leads to clarity in your life.
Challenges are the contrasts that help you identify
what you want and don't want.
Who you are and who you are not.
What is important and what is not.

Life is perfect,
even if your interpretation of it
is imperfect.

When you exercise your
spiritual muscles,
you strengthen your core values.

Soul-full Thought:

Everything is energy.
Energy cannot be created or destroyed,
it can only be transformed.
You are energy.

That means
you were never created.

You are simply an embodiment of a transformed
energy.

Your life is an experiment.
You are the SOULution.

Trust the process of Life.
Trust your soul!

Destruction is easy.
Any fool can destroy.
It takes a wise, courageous person
to construct.

Construction is an out-picture of an inner vision,
inner contemplation,
self-knowledge,
self-awareness.

Constructing, building, or creating is a willingness
to open to greater possibilities.

A constructive consciousness
empowers you to align
with Creative Life Force.

Trust that all things
are perfectly coming together
to make the idea a reality.

What idea is seeking to be birthed
through and as you,
right now?

Be willing to join forces
with the incredible life-giving creative power
that is within you.

---

1 + 1 = 1

No matter how you
cut it,
slice it
dice it,
debate it,
argue it,
explain it,
divide it,
photoshop it
- fill in the blanks -
We are *all* one!!
Everything and everyone is an expression of the
One – Pure Awareness

---◆---

You are an extension of
all that ever was.
A representation of what is.
A reflection of all that will ever be.

You are the embodiment of All That Is.

---◆---

Divine Dichotomy.

You are here to seek and *be* Truth.
You are both physical and non-physical.
You are the past and the future happening *now*!
Darkness and Light
are the same to God.
You might as well focus
on what brings you joy.

---◆---

Slow down
and
catch up with your blessings.

Be still and know, I AM *is* God!

---◆---

Your willingness to give and receive
is your spiritual stimulus package
from an Inner Re-Source.

Until you learn to embrace
and celebrate *differences*,
you will not fully appreciate unity.

If you don't make an appointment
with yourself regularly
you will be disappointed
with yourself!

Don't run from the darkness.
You are the light!

Open up the pantry of your consciousness.
There is much to feast on and share.
There is always more than enough
to go around.

When you are confident about yourself,
there is no competition.
The belief in yourself
becomes a self-sustaining medicine.
You remember that you are *success-full*.

Life is a tightrope.
Find your balance.

To a logical mind,
a spiritual path can feel like
you are walking on a tightrope
without the handlebars.
In truth, you are walking
on solid, sacred ground.
The perceived fall is a fall
into the hands of the Divine.
Even though you cannot see It,
It is very present,
everywhere.

Fall into the arms of Love
and graduate
to a place in consciousness
where you know
there is truly *no spot* where God is not!

No one wins in war.
(*War - We Are Right.*)
Everyone involved is wounded,
physically, emotionally, and psychologically.
On a soul level,
something dies in those who experience
the ugliness of war . . . of being right.

Choose to be happy, rather than being right.

Just for today, take time to REST . . .
in God.
Just for today
Release Every Stressful Thought - R.E.S.T!

Accept your masculine and feminine energy.
Those who experience you will be lifted up by
your presence.
They will see your true beauty.
A whole, integrated, and centered human being
is attractive.

You are a beauty-full work of (he)art!

Life is not a problem to be solved.
Neither are you.
Life is your friend.

Life is for you.
Not against you.

To criticize or judge others
for their religious or spiritual beliefs
reflects
a lack of understanding
of
God as Oneness.

Are You Crazy Enough To Fall In Love With Love?

A spiritual journey is an adventure of Love.
A journey to re-member your Self as Love.

When Love appears to be absent,
it can feel scary and lonely,
especially if you are relying
only on people, places, and things.

The gateway to living in Love is the heart.
The intelligence of the heart transcends
time and space.
Love is a wholehearted journey,
and Love's invitation is simply
to "*fall*" into Its arms and rise up!

Beyond the masks, shame, guilt, blame, and worry
is pure Love.
"*Falling*" in Love is a choice to re-claim your
innocence/inner-essence.

Love is a response-ability,
and we are all endowed with the ability
to respond to life's circumstances,
with love.
It is a choice.

Fall in Love!

Fear is resisting Life.
Love is accepting Life.

You have the free will to *react*
with fear (resisting what is)
or *respond* with love (allowing what is).

Be care-full.
Love will break you open to your heart desires.
It will break your heart open
and connect you with the deep sacred space within you.
Accept what is, and be free.

Your relationship with loved ones
is a catalyst for a heart expansion.

Each day, wake up
with an intention to know Love in a new way,
to see how Love is going to show up
in your day.

Commit to yielding to the call of Love.
Love is intoxicating.
You will scream, "OMG!!"
As you experience spiritual orgasm
on a regular basis.
You will meet God face to face,
through your relationships and daily interactions.

The JOY of relationships!

Are you crazy enough to fall in love with love?
Are you willing?
Breathe!!

Brace yourself for multiple spiritual orgasms!

Acknowledgments

There is a Powerful Presence that guides, inspires, and sustains all that we are. I am grateful for how this Powerful Presence, (which I call, the Great I Am, Spirit, God, the Most High) has inspired, supported, and strengthened me in all that I Am. I Am grateful for the awareness that I Am one with the Great I Am.

I am eternally grateful for my Ancestors. Thank you for reminding me who I am, whose I am, and who I am here to be - a heart-centered Healer and Teacher.

I would like to thank my dad for your constant encouragement and prayers for the manifestation of this book. Mum, I feel your presence and love every day. I know you are with me and inspiring me to trust myself and move forward. Thank you for helping me understand that the veil between the physical and spiritual realms is thinner than I can imagine and that you are just a thought away.

My Beloved, Kishia, after many close calls, we are finally where we belong, in the arms of love with each other. I am grateful for your love. Thank you for seeing me. Thank you for your constant affirmations.

To my siblings, I am eternally grateful for our relationship. I am thankful for your love, care, and support.

Acknowledgments

I believe in the power of community. This book is the result of what happens when a loving community comes together. It is not possible to thank everyone who influenced the birthing of this book. However, I want to mention some of them. Mona Reeves, Jacquelyn Andrews, and Yvette Bacote thank you for your editing skills and creativity. Thank you to Michelle Lowe, Michael Billups, Christine Gautreaux, and Ore Ogungbayi.

To all my listeners from "Life Conversations Radio" to "Ade Presents... BEing You Podcast" thank you for your constant support. To all the guests that I have had the privilege of interviewing, thank you for sharing your wisdom and inspiring the best in me.

To my mentors and spiritual teachers, Rev. Deborah L. Johnson and Rev. Mary Louise Ruffner. Thank you for shining so bright and helping me find my way.

About The Author

Ade Anifowose
Spiritual Healer and Teacher. Sacred Drummer. Podcaster. Mindset Coach. Certified InterPlay Leader.

For over 20 years, Ade has devoted his life to being both a student and teacher of ancient African wisdom traditions. He is known for his optimism and ability to put people at ease to access their inner wisdom. His unique approach opens the hearts and minds of his clients so they can more easily and effectively approach life head-on.

The philosophy of self-empowerment is the thread that runs through all of Ade's talks, workshops, healing sessions, spiritual gatherings, and podcasts. He offers practical guidance to assist his clients in removing blocks and shifting their perspectives, opening their mindset to new opportunities and possibilities.

Ade's teaching is rooted in the understanding that we are the faces of our ancestors. They live in us and we live in them. He believes that real transformation happens when we are willing to go

About The Author

within and do the necessary healing work. Otherwise, we are simply living from a mindset of separation in the realm of Oneness. Ade says, *"Everything is connected and it all belongs."*

He has a deep passion for helping people connect with their unique sense of self and is dedicated to inspiring people to live from the confidence of their most authentic self.

Ade lives in Leicester, UK. He is currently writing his memoir which chronicles his hero's journey of displacement, belonging, and identity.

His website; TheBusinessOfBeing.com.

Social Media: @LifeCoachAde on YouTube, Facebook, Instagram, and Twitter

Printed in Great Britain
by Amazon